To Alley Oop, the original adorable deplorable.

— EM & TR

Regnery® is a registered trademark of Salem Communications Holding Corporation

Cataloging-in-Publication data on file with the Library of Congress

ISBN: 978-1-62157-938-0
e-book ISBN: 978-1-62157-939-7

Published in the United States by
Regnery Publishing
A Division of Salem Media Group
300 New Jersey Ave NW
Washington, DC 20001
www.Regnery.com

Manufactured in the United States of America

10 9 8 7 6 5 4 3 2 1

Books are available in quantity for promotional or premium use. For information on discounts and terms, please visit our website: www.Regnery.com

DONALD
DRAINS THE
SWAMP!

BY
ERIC METAXAS
& TIM RAGLIN

REGNERY
PUBLISHING
A Division of Salem Media Group

A long, long time ago, there was a kingdom

where everyone lived in caves.

So they called them cavemen.

But the King of all the cavemen went to live

in a white castle in the middle of a swamp, far, far away.

So because he never saw or talked with the people he ruled,

he forgot all about them — and all the people were sad.

Among them lived a famous caveman named Donald.

Donald loved to build caves.

In fact, everyone wanted a cave built by Donald.

One day a group of people came to Donald.

They were very upset.

"Come in," Donald said. "Have a seat.

What is on your mind?"

"The King has forgotten all about us!" they said.

Donald nodded. "I've noticed."

"We tried to talk to the King,

but the creatures who live in the swamp take up all his time.

We try to get his attention, but they always stop us.

Would you talk to the King and ask him to help us?"

"I can try," Donald said.

"But you know you'll have

to get past the swamp creatures!"

"They're slippery!"

"— and scaly!"

"— and SLIMY!"

"I think I can handle them," Donald said.

"Maybe I'll wear gloves."

So the next day, Donald traveled to the edge of the swamp.

The first swamp creature he met was a Lobby-o-saurus.

"Hello," Donald said.

"Hello," said the Lobby-o-saurus.

15

"I need to speak with the King!" said Donald.

"The people he rules over need his help."

"It doesn't work that way," said the Lobby-o-saurus.

"The King only helps those of us who live in the swamp.

That's the way it's always been.

Would you like to live in the swamp?

Maybe I can arrange something."

"No, thanks," said Donald. "I don't care for the swamp."

"How rude!" said the Lobby-o-saurus.

"You should be more diplomatic."

"I'm very sorry," said Donald.

"I don't like you much either."

Donald then tried speaking to other swamp creatures.

But they were all the same. Sad!

Donald went back to see his friends.

"I'm sorry," Donald said, "but it's even worse than I thought."

"What do you mean?" everyone asked

"I mean, we're going to have to get drastic," he said.

"How drastic?"

Donald looked them in the eyes.

"We've got to... DRAIN... THE... SWAMP!" he said.

Everyone gasped.

"You shouldn't say that!" someone said.

"Yes," said another. "The swamp creatures might get angry."

Donald smiled.

"You've all been angry for a long time.

Maybe it's their turn."

But some of the people didn't believe he could do it.

"No one can drain the swamp!" they said.

"It's IMPOSSIBLE!"

A lot of the cavemen thought Donald was crazy

and they walked away, muttering.

"You shouldn't have said that!" said Donald.

"When someone tells me something's impossible,

I won't stop until it's done."

But others stuck around. "Go, Donald! Go!" they said.

"You can do it! Drain the swamp!

DRAIN THE SWAMP!"

But how WOULD he do it?

No one could figure out how.

But Donald knew how.

He'd done many things like this before.

"It's simple," he said. "We just need to make a way

for the swamp water to escape!

We'll dig a trench!"

"It will be the BEST, BIGGEST trench you've ever seen!

It'll be HUGE!"

And we'll even come in below budget!"

So the next day Donald went to the edge of the swamp.

He put down his club and picked up a shovel and

began to dig.

When all the swamp creatures saw him, they were furious!

"What do you think you're doing?" they demanded.

"ARE YOU CRAZY?"

Donald smiled. "I'm digging a trench.

It will be the BEST, BIGGEST trench you've ever seen!

And it will drain the swamp!"

"You're mean!" they said.

"We need this swamp! Where will we live?"

"I can build you a nice cave, near where I live.

Lots of us live there," he said.

"ECHHH!" They said.

"We can't stand the people

who live outside the swamp!"

"They're uneducated!"

"— they're uncultured!"

" — they're DEPLORABLE!"

But Donald wasn't listening.

He knew he had a job to do.

So he just kept digging.

Then he noticed something he'd never seen before!

The green color of the swamp water looked strange.

It wasn't a normal swamp color at all!

It was the color of money!

In fact, it *was* money!

The whole swamp was filled with money!

As far as the eye could see!

Now Donald knew why all the swamp creatures lived there.

Then Donald saw something huge out of the corner of his

eye. It was the biggest swamp creature of them all.

It was a monster called the George-o-saurus!

"Now you've really done it," the swamp creatures shouted.

"You've made the George-o-saurus mad!"

"NOT AS MAD AS YOU MADE US!" came a shout.

Donald turned to see all the people who lived outside

the swamp. They'd come to help!

They were all armed with shovels.

"DRAIN THE SWAMP!" they shouted. "DRAIN THE SWAMP!"

Suddenly they were all digging alongside Donald.

Because there were so many of them,

the trench was dug quickly.

And in a moment, the swamp water began to drain!

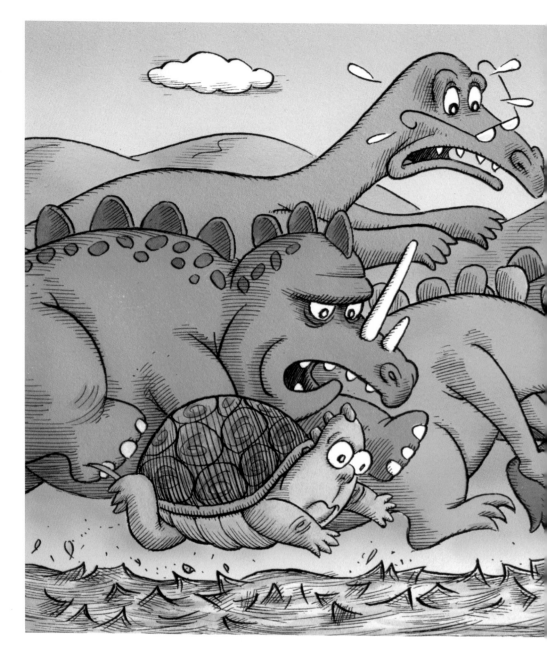

The swamp creatures couldn't believe their eyes!

They began to shriek in horror!

Then they ran toward the trench.

But they didn't stop!

They just kept going —

chasing the money flowing out of the swamp!

Even the King chased the money!

And the George-o-saurus too!

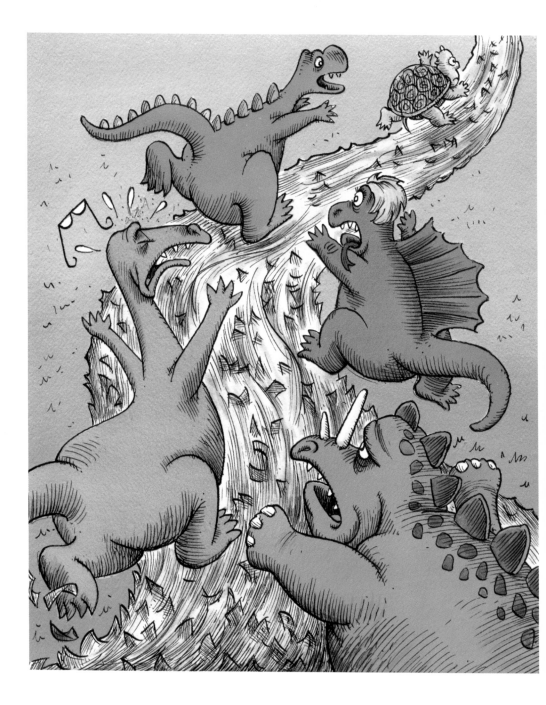

But the money flowed away so fast and so far

that all those chasing it were never, ever seen again!

All the people cheered.

Once the swamp was drained, everything looked different.

It was beautiful. Flowers bloomed and trees grew.

But after all that, the people still couldn't talk to the King.

What was the point of all they had done?

Then a little girl had an idea.

"What if Donald were our new King?" she asked.

"Donald," everyone shouted, "would you be our new King?

And live in the castle?

And let us talk to you when we have a problem?"

"You don't need a King," Donald said.

"You're free now!

A King orders his people around.

But whoever leads a free people,

has to take *his* orders from *them*!"

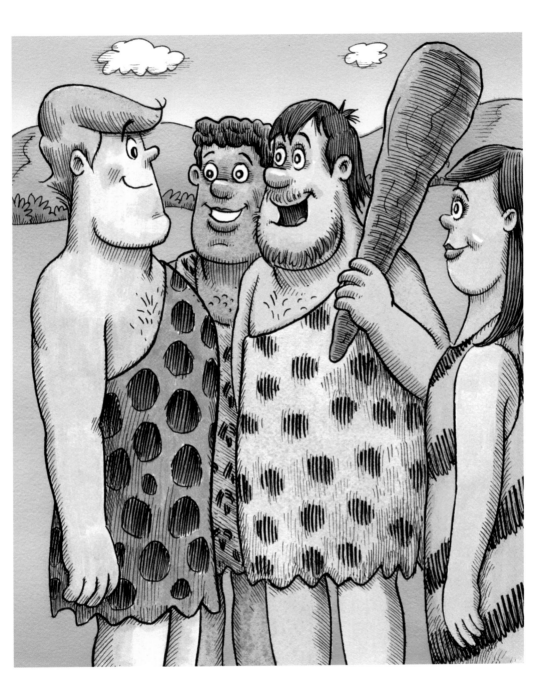

"You mean like a president?"

"Sure. And if that's what you're looking for, I guess...

I'm your caveman!" Everyone cheered.

The people gave Donald a special outfit

that represented their newfound freedom.

So Donald and his family went to live in the castle.

He did some remodeling, but he kept it under budget.

And the people lived happily ever after.

Bigly.

Photo © Josh Del

ERIC METAXAS

ERIC METAXAS has written over thirty children's
books, including the bestsellers *Squanto and the Miracle of
Thanksgiving* and *It's Time to Sleep, My Love,* illustrated by
Nancy Tillman. He has also been a writer for *VeggieTales.*

Since editing the *Yale Record*, the nation's oldest college humor magazine, Eric's humor has appeared in *The New Yorker* and *The Atlantic*. Woody Allen has called these pieces "quite funny." Eric wrote a full-length book parody of the Ripley's "Believe It or Not" books, titled *Don't You Believe It!*, prompting novelist Mark Helprin to call him "the thinking man's Gary Larson (*The Far Side*)."

Metaxas is the bestselling author of *Bonhoeffer: Pastor, Martyr, Prophet, Spy* and many other books, including *Martin Luther, If You Can Keep It, Miracles, Seven Women, Seven Men,* and *Amazing Grace*. His books have been translated into more than twenty-five languages.

He is the host of the *Eric Metaxas Show*, a nationally syndicated radio program heard on more than 300 stations around the US, featuring in-depth interviews with a wide variety of guests.

Metaxas was the keynote speaker at the 2012 National Prayer Breakfast in Washington, D.C., an event attended by the president and first lady, the vice president, members of Congress, and other US and world leaders.

ABC News has called him a "photogenic, witty ambassador for faith in public life," and *The Indianapolis Star* described him as "a Protestant version of William F. Buckley." Metaxas's *Wall Street Journal* op-ed, "Science Increasingly Makes the Case for God" is the most popular and shared piece in the history of the *Journal*.

Metaxas has been featured as a cultural commentator on CNN, MSNBC, and Fox News programs and has been interviewed about his work on the *Today Show, Fox and Friends, The History Channel*, and C-SPAN. He has been featured on many radio programs, including NPR's *Morning Edition* and *Talk of the Nation*, as well as *The Hugh Hewitt Show, The Dennis Prager Show,* and *The Michael Medved Show*.

Metaxas is a Senior Fellow at the King's College in New York City. He lives in Manhattan with his wife and daughter.

TIM RAGLIN

TIM RAGLIN was born and raised in Independence, Kansas, and earned a degree from Washington University's School of Fine Arts in St. Louis. He then immediately launched into the world of freelance illustration, first in St. Louis, then in New York.

Raglin has illustrated many children's picture books, the most popular being *Deputy Dan* and the *Five Funny Frights* series, each having sold over two million copies. He has also worked with Rabbit Ears Productions, a children's video company, and illustrated several of Rudyard Kipling's *Just So Stories*, including the Grammy Award-winning *The Elephant's Child*. Raglin also illustrated and directed his own version of *Pecos Bill*, which won both a Grammy Award for Best Children's Recording and a Parent's Choice Classic Award. Tim served as the creative director of Rabbit Ears until 1991.

He has since illustrated a number of children's picture books, including *The Thirteen Days of Halloween*, *The Wolf Who Cried Boy*, *Twelfth Night*, and *Go Track a Yak!*. But Raglin's chief focus has been his work as the publisher of several of his own picture books, including *Uncle Mugsy* and *The Terrible Twins of Christmas*, which received a Silver Medal from the New York Society of Illustrators. He also published *The Birthday ABC*, which was chosen as an American Library Association "Pick of the List" book in 1995. He is currently working on several new picture books, which he plans to publish under his own imprint, the first of which will be *The Curse of Catunkhamun*.

Raglin has had a number of books chosen to appear in The Original Art Show: The Best in Children's Books, as well as the New York Society's Annual Show. He lives in Independence, Kansas.